Withdrawn

Angela
MERKEL

Claire Throp

Raintree is an imprint of Capstone Global Library Limited, a company incorporated in England and Wales having its registered office at 7 Pilgrim Street, London, EC4V 6LB – Registered company number: 6695582

www.raintreepublishers.co.uk
myorders@raintreepublishers.co.uk

Text © Capstone Global Library Limited 2014
First published in hardback in 2014
The moral rights of the proprietor have been asserted.

Edited by Nick Hunter, James Benefield, and Abby Colich
Designed by Philippa Jenkins
Picture research by Ruth Blair
Production by Helen McCreath
Originated by Capstone Global Library Ltd
Printed and bound in China

ISBN 978 406 27396 0
17 16 15 14 13
10 9 8 7 6 5 4 3 2 1

British Library Cataloguing in Publication Data
A full catalogue record for this book is available from the British Library.

Acknowledgements
We would like to thank the following for permission to reproduce photographs: Corbis pp. 5 (© ARND WIEGMANN/Reuters), pp. 7, 8 (© Ossenbrink Media Group/Sygma), 12 (© Reuters), 19 (© WOLFGANG RATTAY/Reuters), 27 (© KAI PFAFFENBACH/Reuters), 28 (© Michael Kappeler/dpa), 38 (© Stathis/Demotix), 41 (© JULIEN WARNAND/epa); Getty Images pp. 4 (Kevork Djansezian), 9 (Gamma-Keystone), 14 (Richard Ellis), pp. 16, 17, 18, 23 (Ulrich Baumgarten), 20 (Patrick PIEL/Gamma-Rapho), 21 (Topical Press Agency), 22 (ERIC FEFERBERG/AFP), 25 (Jose Giribas/Bloomberg), 26 (ROLAND MAGUNIA/AFP), 29 (Pete Souza/The White House), 30 (Brendan Smialowski), 31 (Franziska Krug), 32 (NATALIA KOLESNIKOVA/AFP0), 33 (Tim Graham), 35 (Uriel Sinai), 36 (DANIEL ROLAND/AFP), 37 (Sean Gallup), 39 (SAUL LOEB/AFP), 42 (THIERRY CHARLIER/AFP), 43 (Sean Gallup); Getty Images/Eirini Vourloumis/Bloomberg p. 40; Photoshot pp. 13 (© Imago), 34; Superstock pp. 11 (Thomas Robbin/ imagebroker.net), 15 (© Denis Lazarenko), 24 (imagebroker.net).

Cover photograph of Angela Merkel giving a press conference at the Chancellery in Berlin, reproduced with the permission of Getty Images (JOHANNES EISELE/AFP).

Every effort has been made to contact copyright holders of material reproduced in this book. Any omissions will be rectified in subsequent printings if notice is given to the publisher.

CONTENTS

Some words are shown in bold, **like this**. You can
find out what they mean by looking in the glossary.

A strong woman

It was 1998. Everything was going well for Angela Merkel. She had been promoted twice in her brief political career for the party in power in Germany, the Christian Democratic Union (CDU). She was feeling positive. Then the CDU lost the **general election**. After 16 years of the party being in power, it came as a shock. It also seemed like Merkel had lost her job.

Angela had been Minister for the Environment. However, she was soon given another job: secretary-general of the CDU. But then, in 1999, there was another shock. Helmut Kohl, the previous chancellor and honorary chairman of the CDU, admitted receiving illegal **campaign** money and placing it in a secret bank account. The CDU was fined 41 million marks (about £17.5 million) and was nearly **bankrupt**.

Angela is one of the few women leaders in the world. Here, she talks with fellow leaders at the NATO summit in 2012.

Many CDU members stayed loyal to Kohl, but not Angela. She wanted the truth. When she found it, she wrote an article for a newspaper criticizing Kohl. Some party members disapproved, but others were impressed with her honesty and courage. In April 2000, the party chose Angela Merkel as their next leader. After only 11 years in politics, Angela was the leader of one of the biggest political parties in Germany.

Angela's rise to power

In 2002, Angela did not receive quite enough support to run as chancellor. But, in 2005, she became the country's leader. Angela's rise from a **pastor's** daughter in East Germany to the first female chancellor may seem meteoric. But it was the result of extremely hard work.

Fact:
The CDU is one of the main political parties in Germany. In some ways, it is similar to the Conservative Party in the UK.

Childhood

Angela Merkel was born Angela Dorothea Kasner on 17 July 1954 in Hamburg, West Germany. Angela's father, Horst, was a pastor in the Protestant church. Her mother, Herlind, was an English and Latin teacher. Shortly after her birth, Angela's family moved to a small village called Quitzow in Brandenburg, in East Germany. This was unusual at the time, as Germany was a divided country. There were restrictions on crossing between East and West.

This map shows the main places mentioned in this book, as well as how Germany was divided into East and West during the years 1949–1990.

Hamburg

Quitzow Templin

■ Berlin

G E R M A N Y

Frankfurt

German Democratic Republic (East Germany)

Federal Republic of Germany (West Germany)

Stuttgart

Munich

N

0   150 kilometres

0   100 miles

Angela is seen here at the age of one.

Happy childhood

Angela was three years old when the family moved to Templin, a small city in Brandenburg. Her brother, Marcus, was born in July 1957. Angela's parents were very strict. They taught Angela to work hard and always strive to be the best. In 1964, Angela's sister, Irene, was born.

THEN and NOW

A divided country

A few years after losing World War II (1939–1945), Germany was divided into two states: the German Democratic Republic (East Germany) and the Federal Republic of Germany (West Germany). East Germany was closely connected to the Soviet Union, which was dominated by **communism**. In this political system, all property and major industry is owned by the state. It results in a loss of freedom for ordinary people. In contrast, West Germany became a successful **democracy**. Within 20 years it was one of the richest nations in the world. In 1990, East and West Germany were reunited.

Angela is seen here in 1958. She was a shy child who preferred reading to sport.

A family divided

Angela's mother's family was separated by the Berlin Wall when Angela was only seven.

"Seeing the grown-ups around me, even my parents, so stunned that they actually broke out in tears, was something that shook me to the core."

The Berlin Wall

Angela grew up at a time when the eyes of the world were on East Germany. About 2.5 million East Germans fled to West Germany via the city of Berlin between 1949 and 1961. In 1961, the Berlin Wall was built to separate East Berlin from West Berlin. People could no longer travel freely between East and West.

School days

Angela was excellent in almost all subjects at school except sport. Learning Russian was **compulsory** in East Germany. Angela did so well at it that she won a trip to Moscow in the Soviet Union.

Living under communism

Like many other teenagers, Angela joined the FDJ (Freie Deutsche Jugend, or, in English, Free German Youth), the communist youth organization. It was necessary to join if you wanted to go to university. Angela and her father were also asked to spy on their neighbours by the Stasi, the German secret police. Both Angela and her father refused.

The building of the Berlin Wall divided the city of Berlin in two. A barrier was erected along the rest of the border between East and West Germany.

Was Angela a communist?

Critics have suggested that Angela's family were at least sympathetic to communism if not actual communists. Her biographer Gerd Langguth said in 2005,

> "She was never convinced by communism as an idea ... But she didn't fight the system either."

Before politics

Angela's school marks were so good that she was one of the 5 per cent of German students who qualified for a full university education. In 1973, Angela began to study physics at the University of Leipzig. She met fellow student Ulrich Merkel during an exchange trip to Russia. They got married in 1977. They moved to East Berlin and Angela worked as a researcher in a laboratory at the Central Institute for Physical Chemistry at the Academy of Sciences. Angela and Ulrich's marriage did not last and they separated in 1981. Divorce followed in 1982, but Angela kept Ulrich's surname.

Free German Youth

During the 1980s, Angela became more politically involved in the FDJ movement. She soon became Secretary of Political Education, which Angela has since argued just meant organizing tickets and events. However, some people have said that it was a more important role and that it suggests Angela might have been an enthusiastic communist.

No one is completely certain how far Angela's involvement in FDJ went, but Angela herself has downplayed it.

Educational success

Angela received her PhD in 1986. A PhD (also known as a doctorate) is the highest qualification in education a person can achieve, and is usually studied at a university. Angela then moved to a different chemistry department within the Academy of Sciences. She continued to work there until 1990.

Angela studied physics and physical chemistry at the University of Leipzig.

Fact:
A number of articles co-authored by Angela have been published in respected international scientific journals. In 1998, for example, she published an article about environmental ethics in the journal *Science*.

A new direction

On 9 November 1989, East Germans were once more free to travel to West Berlin. They began to tear at the Berlin Wall with their bare hands. What started as a few people soon became many. This was the day the wall fell.

A new world opens up

The events of 1989 had a huge impact on the lives of East Germans. Angela said of this time,

"My life changed completely ... with the fall of the [Berlin] wall."

The fall of the Berlin Wall really opened up the possibilities in Angela's mind of what she could do with her life.

Angela is seen here at the Berlin Wall East Side Gallery, which is seen as a monument to freedom.

Angela walked into West Berlin on that day. She has said, "The biggest surprise of my life was freedom … Once you've had such a wonderful surprise in your life, then you think anything is possible." She decided then and there to play a part in the reconstruction of Germany. Soon after, Angela joined the **opposition** party in East Germany, the Democratic Awakening (DA).

Democratic Awakening

The DA was set up by East German church leaders to push through reunification. Angela's family knew one of them – Lothar de Maizière. It was partly through this connection that Angela became the DA spokesperson when the party won the first – and last – democratic elections in East Germany.

Shortly before reunification, the DA became part of the Christian Democractic Union (CDU). Chancellor Helmut Kohl supported the East German CDU, so Angela decided to join them.

THEN and NOW

Reunification
German states had first been united in 1871, under Kaiser (Emperor) Wilhelm I. Then defeat in World War II divided the country. After the fall of the Berlin Wall in 1989, Berlin became the capital city of Germany. Reunification became official on 3 October 1990.

13

Elected!

The first general election in the unified Germany took place in December 1990. Angela was quite well known as the spokesperson for the old East German government. She campaigned for a seat in the Bundestag (parliament) and was elected for the **constituency** of Stralsund-Rügen-Grimmen in north-east Germany.

Promotion

Angela was promoted quickly, partly because Chancellor Kohl wanted East German representation in his government. He may also have thought she would be quite easy to control. The first of two major promotions came in 1991 when she was made Minister for Women and Youth. During her time as minister, she was responsible for pushing through the Equal Opportunities Act, which supported more family-friendly workplaces. It also improved educational opportunities for women.

Helmut Kohl had been elected chancellor in 1982. He described Angela as *das Mädchen* ("the girl") because she was the youngest member of the cabinet.

The Bundestag meet in the Reichstag building in Berlin.

The German political system

Every few years, people in Germany vote for which party they want to represent them in the Bundestag. Many of the political parties in Germany are small. Therefore, two or more parties often join together to form a **coalition**. This means the governing party gains a majority of seats in the Bundestag. The CDU and Christian Social Union (CSU) campaign together. The CDU's main rivals are the Social Democratic Party (abbreviated in Germany to the SPD). The Free Democratic Party (FDP) and the Green Party are the other main parties.

The chancellor is the leader of the government. The president suggests someone for chancellor and members of the Bundestag then vote on whether that person should be elected.

BREAKING BOUNDARIES

PAVING THE WAY

Angela is a Protestant woman from East Germany, which is unusual for a Christian Democrat politician. The CDU is traditionally dominated by Catholic men from West Germany.

15

More promotions

Angela was voted Deputy Chairwoman, the second in command of the CDU, in December 1991, winning 86.4 per cent of the vote. Kohl said that the party needed to focus more on three sections of society that Angela represented: former East Germans, women, and young people. She was only 37 at the time and much younger than many other leaders in the party.

Angela was sworn in as Minister for the Environment, Nature Conservation, and Nuclear Safety on 17 November 1994.

BREAKING BOUNDARIES

A DIFFERENT APPROACH

Most members of the CDU are in finance, law, or business. Angela has a very different background. She is a scientist and likes to think carefully about issues. She looks at them from all sides before making a decision. Trial and error is important in a scientist's work – if something doesn't work, he or she will try a different approach. Angela's turnaround on the issue of nuclear energy is an example (see page 37).

Angela's role as Minister for the Environment brought her into the public eye like never before.

Criticism

Then, in 1994, Angela was appointed Minister for the Environment, Nature Conservation, and Nuclear Safety, at least partly because of her science background. The environment is an issue close to Angela's heart, but her ideas were criticised for not being powerful enough. However, she did manage to push through a number of recycling programmes. Angela also tried to make the environmental issue a Europe-wide one. She pushed for the creation of the Kyoto Protocol to try to cut greenhouse gases. She suggested that a tax to help cut greenhouse gas emissions should be placed on regions rather than countries. This would mean that no single country's economy would be too badly affected.

The nuclear waste issue

Angela was heavily criticised for her role in the nuclear waste issue of 1995. Nuclear power stations produce radioactive waste that is extremely harmful. Nobody really knows how to get rid of it safely. Most countries choose to bury it deep underground. Germany stored its waste in a town called Gorleben. It was transported by train in steel-lined boxes that protesters claimed were leaking. The protesters tried to block the railway and police had to remove them. They did this with dogs and water cannons. The violence upset many people. Angela was held responsible and accused of not caring about the health of the German people.

Angela remained calm. She pointed out that there was no evidence for health problems. She was able to survive the potential crisis.

Shock result

Helmut Kohl had been chancellor since 1982, but in 1998 his party, the CDU, lost the election. The SPD joined with the Green Party to run the country. It was a huge shock.

Gerhard Schröder, leader of the SPD, is seen here celebrating the 1998 election win.

In 1998, Angela married Joachim Sauer –
her second marriage. It is claimed they only
married because of pressure from the CDU; it
was not appropriate for the deputy leader of
the conservative CDU to be only living with
someone rather than married to them.

BREAKING BOUNDARIES

CHALLENGING PREJUDICE

The CDU is known as the "party of the family". But Angela has been divorced
and has no children. If men do not have children, it is not usually a media
issue, but for women it can be. Much has been made of Angela not having
children. Some have suggested that because her experience is different from
most women, she cannot expect to know what's right for them.

Rising to the top

Things went from bad to worse for the CDU in late 1999 and early 2000. Wolfgang Schäuble had replaced Helmut Kohl as leader of the CDU in 1998. Kohl now also had to resign as chairman of the party after admitting he had illegally accepted contributions to the party. Schäuble then had to resign over his own handling of the situation.

Staying tough

Angela can be **ruthless** when people have displeased her, as seen with Helmut Kohl. Constanze Stelzenmüller, of the German Marshall Fund, said,

"She does not like the established CDU politicians, mainly businessmen, with their sense of entitlement [feeling they have a right to power]."

Angela's rise in politics continued after key members of the CDU had to resign.

THEN and NOW

Women and the vote

There are a number of women leaders around the world in the 21st century. However, in many countries it has been fewer than 100 years since women gained the right to vote. Women who fought for the right to vote were called suffragettes. In the UK, women over 30 who owned property could vote from 1918. It was 1928 before all women had equal voting rights with men. In Germany, it was 1918. Women in other countries have had to wait longer – for example, Bangladesh in 1972 and Switzerland in 1971. In Saudi Arabia, women will be able to vote from 2015.

Women around the world wanted voting rights
Here, women in Britain protest in three languages.

Angela had written a newspaper article critcizing Kohl. This angered some of Kohl's supporters. Kohl had promoted Angela several times and they thought she had betrayed him. For Angela, however, the truth was more important. Her courage in standing up for her beliefs was rewarded with her being elected president of the CDU in April 2000.

Changes

Angela knew that everyone would be watching to see how the party got through the crisis. She made immediate changes such as cutting costs on food and publications, and cutting jobs. Rather than the lavish dinner parties Kohl used to hold for the party, Angela's dinner party meals consisted of cold meat, cabbage, and potatoes!

Angela decided to focus on policies such as letting competition, rather than government interference, decide which businesses would survive. She emphasized her version of Christian values such as freedom and equality, which could help give people "a sense of their roots".

Angela supported Edmund Stoiber in his attempt to become chancellor. Many in her party did not forget this willingness to work for the party rather than herself.

Missed out

In 2002, Angela deliberated too long about whether to stand for nomination to become a **candidate** for chancellor. The leader of the coalition party, the CSU, was Edmund Stoiber. He decided to challenge Angela for the role of chancellor. She realized she did not have much support from her own party. So Angela pulled out of the race and instead gave her support to Stoiber. Unfortunately, he lost the election and Gerhard Schröder of the opposing SPD party was re-elected. This meant that Angela became leader of the opposition in the Bundestag.

A new type of politician

Angela had lots of support from her party, despite not running for chancellor in 2002. CDU member Hannelore Heuser said of her in 2000,

"To me, Ms Merkel is about a new style in politics, one that is honest, direct, and clear. That is the most drastic and significant change after what we now perceive [see] as the dangerous murkiness of the Kohl system."

Building support

Angela worked hard over the next few years to build support for the CDU. The party won a number of regional elections in 2003. In May 2005, it won local elections in states where it had not won for nearly 40 years. This prompted Gerhard Schröder to call for an early general election. He had decided that he could beat Angela, but, like many others, he had **underestimated** her.

Angela's campaigning made sure that the CDU would challenge Schröder and his party at the next election.

Modern campaigning allows for photos of candidates to appear everywhere, including on the side of a bus!

Deutschlands
Chancen nutzen."

Campaigning

Angela stood for the need to make changes in Germany's governing style. This meant businesses could be free of interference from the government. Angela also stated that the government would be friendlier towards the United States. The United States was disliked as a result of the Iraq war, but Angela suggested that the war's goals – including to overthrow Saddam Hussein – were correct.

Fact:
Newspapers at the time of the campaign tried to show the private side of Angela. She was seen gardening and jogging, and was said to enjoy films starring Dustin Hoffman.

Losing ground

During the campaign, Angela stuck to talking about problems and how they could be solved. Other candidates, particularly Gerhard Schröder, were more vague about their policies. They attacked Angela for being boring and not smiling enough for the voters. The CDU was leading the polls by 18 per cent near the start of the campaign. By the time of the election, its lead had dropped. Schröder's criticisms about Angela may have contributed to the loss of its previously large lead.

General election 2005

In September 2005, the CDU/CSU won the general election with a very small **margin**. Neither the CDU/CSU nor the SPD had a majority of seats in the Bundestag. This meant the two parties were forced into a coalition together. A coalition has to have at least 50 per cent of the seats in the Bundestag. It took many days to work out which party would get which **cabinet** posts. Someone also had to be **nominated** as chancellor. After nearly three weeks of talks, Angela was put forward as the candidate for chancellor of a CDU and SPD coalition.

Angela's supporters affectionately call her Angie.

Chancellor at last

The candidate for chancellor must win a majority of the votes available. The chancellor then holds their position for four years. Angela was voted in as chancellor on 22 November 2005. She got 397 votes out of a possible 614. However, 51 members of the coalition refused to vote or voted against her. Clearly, not everyone was a fan. However, the vote is carried out in secret. This meant that it was not possible to know who exactly chose not to support her.

In November 2005, Angela became Germany's eighth chancellor since World War II.

Outside politics

One of the reasons that so many German people like Angela is because she appears "normal". She does not have a celebrity lifestyle and can sometimes be seen shopping for dinner, directly after meetings with important political leaders.

Angela and the Swedish Prime Minister Fredrik Reinfelt (right) support their teams at a match between Germany and Sweden in 2012.

Substance over style

When she first entered politics, many thought that Angela's dowdy image would make her unpopular:

"German voters aren't stupid – they don't want a Britney Spears as the chancellor of Germany, they want a serious leader whom they can trust. Angela knows what she's doing."

Detmar Doering,
the head of the Liberal Institute in Potsdam

Angela, UK Prime Minister David Cameron, and US President Barack Obama were at the **G8 summit meeting** in the United States in 2012 when the Champions League final was on.

Football

Angela is a huge football fan. She tries to attend Germany's matches whenever her political schedule allows. She can often be seen cheering them on enthusiastically. Angela has even dined out with the national team!

Angela's husband

Angela's husband Joachim Sauer is a quantum chemist. They met in the mid-1980s when he was her mentor as she worked on her PhD. The couple lived together for many years before getting married in 1998. Sauer comes from the former East Germany and has two children from a previous marriage. He doesn't like being in the public eye, so did not attend her **inauguration** as chancellor. Instead, he watched it on TV.

Fact:
Angela is famous for her home-made plum cake. She is often asked by journalists if she has had time to make a plum cake recently!

29

Sense of humour

Many of Angela's critics say she doesn't show emotion or have a sense of humour. Those who know her well say that is not true. She is great at telling jokes and funny stories.

In 2011, at a lunch held in Angela's honour in the United States, she made a presentation to Hillary Clinton, who was US Secretary of State at the time. The gift was a framed German newspaper showing a picture of the midsections of the two women standing next to each other. The newspaper was suggesting that you couldn't tell the two women apart. There was much laughter as Angela pointed out the "guess who?" riddle of the photograph.

Hillary Clinton, the US Secretary of State, saw the funny side of Angela's gift.

Angela's husband, Joachim Sauer, is not often seen in public with Angela, but here they are attending the Bayreuth Festival in 2012.

Other interests

Angela loves classical music and goes to concerts with friends whenever possible. She tries to attend the Bayreuth Festival (a festival of music by German composer Richard Wagner) with her husband every year.

Angela also enjoys reading, gardening, cooking, and going on hiking holidays in the Alps. She has said that she is most happy in the countryside. Whenever she has any free time she goes for walks with her husband around Uckermark, near where she grew up.

Fact:
On Angela Merkel's own website, she says what she would like to do if she had more time: "I've got one big dream: to travel from Moscow to Vladivostok on the Trans-Siberian Railway." The Trans-Siberian Railway is the longest railway in the world at 9,441 kilometres (5,867 miles).

Life as chancellor

Angela's first real test as chancellor came at the **European Union (EU)** summit meeting in December 2005. France and the UK were arguing over the EU budget. It emerged that the person who calmed things down was Angela Merkel. She helped the leaders to a **compromise** on the budget. Her **analytical skills** and **diplomacy** were vital.

Speaking out

Angela has visited many world leaders to strengthen international partnerships. She made a mark in several countries by not being afraid to speak her mind. She criticized the United States for their treatment of prisoners at Guantanámo Bay, a prison for terrorist suspects. At the 2006 G8 summit, Angela criticized the host nation, Russia, on both its electoral system and its interruptions to energy supply. Russia has large natural gas reserves and wanted Ukraine to pay more to use them. When the country refused, Russia cut off the energy supply. But it also affected supply to other countries.

Angela's comments about Russia were not all bad. She also reported that the G8 summit had an "open and honest atmosphere".

THEN and NOW

The iron ladies

Angela is often compared to Margaret Thatcher, the UK's first and, so far, only woman prime minister. Margaret Thatcher won leadership of the Conservative Party in 1975 and then became prime minister in 1979. Angela has even been given the same nickname of the Iron Lady. They do have similar histories – Thatcher also had a science background. She studied chemistry at Oxford, and her father was the dominant person in the household. While things may have improved for women in many areas of life, a lot has remained the same. For example, there remains a strong focus on what women look like: both Thatcher and Angela had hair and clothing makeovers when they came to power and newspapers sometimes write more about what they have worn than what they have done as politicians.

Global financial crisis

The global financial crisis began in 2007. Banks around the world were running out of money and were unable to borrow any more. The banks had to be bailed out, or rescued, with loans of money from the governments. In October 2008, this happened to one of Germany's largest banks. The following month, the country was declared to be in recession. Recession is when a country's economy stops growing and shrinks for a period of time. This means a fall in income and spending and, often, more people losing their jobs.

Angela's relationship with former French President Nicolas Sarkozy has been an up-and-down one.

Angela lays a wreath in memory of the Jews killed by the Nazis during World War II. Israeli Prime Minister Ehud Olmet stands behind her in the Hall of Remembrance at the Yad Vashem Holocaust Memorial in Jerusalem, Israel.

Contrasting solutions

Many countries such as the UK and the United States set up spending programmes that they thought would help people to get through the crisis. Angela was one of the few leaders who did not want to increase government spending to solve the problem – she felt that it would only make things worse. She said: "We have to have the courage to swim against the tide." At the time, Germany was the strongest EU economy, with a balanced budget and good employment figures.

35

Re-election

Angela was re-elected as chancellor in 2009. This time, the CDU/CSU partnership formed a coalition government with the FDP. The FDP is a party more like the CDU because it also believes in a free market.

In November 2010, Angela won re-election as leader of the CDU with 90.4 per cent of the vote. She had given a strong speech at the CDU party conference that won a 10-minute standing ovation. Angela's biographer, Gerd Langguth, said, "It was a passionate and polarizing speech, quite out of character. By stressing her party's Christian roots, Chancellor Angela is trying to win back some of the core conservative voters who've drifted away."

Angela Merkel waves after being re-elected as party leader during the CDU party conference in Karlsruhe, Germany.

Angela's law

Some people say that Angela changes policy because of her science background. In other words, she doesn't want to make a decision until she is absolutely certain about it. Opposition leader Frank-Walter Steinmeier describes this as something he calls Angela's Law:

"The more fiercely Angela rules something out, the more certain it is that she will eventually adopt that policy."

Angela faced suspicion when she changed her mind about nuclear energy. Some thought it was related to winning votes ahead of an upcoming election.

Angela and the environment

Angela is the only leader of a large wealthy nation that has proposed major policy on slowing greenhouse gas emissions. Angela plans that 45 per cent of Germany's electricity will come from renewable energy by 2030.

One of the major issues of Angela's chancellorship has been nuclear energy. She went against public opinion in 2010. She announced that nuclear plants would be phased out in 14 years. However, after the Japanese Fukushima nuclear disaster of March 2011, she changed her mind and moved the deadline to 2020 or earlier.

Eurozone crisis

Countries of the EU that have the euro as their currency are known as the Eurozone. Some Eurozone governments had got into a lot of debt. Greece's debt was much larger than anyone realized. It could not afford to pay back the money it owed and had to be bailed out, or rescued, by Eurozone countries with stronger economies. In return, it was forced to agree to **austerity** measures. These involved reducing government spending and increasing **taxes**. Many of the cuts affected public services such as healthcare and education. Many people lost their jobs, while others suffered pay cuts. This led to rioting in Greece and Portugal.

The people of Athens, Greece, were angry at the austerity measures put in place. Many rioted as a result.

Angela was given the US Presidential Medal of Freedom in June 2011. It is the highest **civilian** honour in the United States.

Foreign recognition

When Angela was given the US Presidential Medal of Freedom, US President Barack Obama said,

"Tonight, we honour Angela Merkel not for being denied her freedom, or even for attaining her freedom, but for what she achieved when she gained her freedom."

He was talking about Angela using her position as one of the most powerful women in the world to fight for everyone's right to freedom.

United front

In May 2010, Angela and French President Nicolas Sarkozy united to say that something had to be done to prevent the crisis in Greece from affecting other countries. They suggested rules to limit government spending. Later in the year, a permanent fund for dealing with major debt was agreed at a Eurozone summit meeting.

Angela's turnaround

Angela has been criticized for changing her mind about how to deal with the Eurozone crisis. At first, she was very tough when negotiating an aid package with the International Monetary Fund. Many Germans were annoyed at having to rescue countries that had spent without thinking of the consequences. But as things got worse, Angela agreed to more generous aid packages, which angered Germans even more. In July 2011, Angela had to defend her support of a second bailout of Greece. Now some Germans believe she is being too **lenient** towards struggling countries.

The people of Greece were not pleased to see Angela when she visited their country in October 2012. They created an image of her as a clown or joker-like figure.

Saving the Eurozone

Angela spoke about the financial crisis during an interview with the BBC in March 2012:

"We have taken the decision to be in a currency union ... It would be catastrophic if we were to say to one of those who have decided to be with us: 'We no longer want you'."

Angela was explaining that she did not want Greece to leave the Eurozone. She was sure that Germany would do everything it could to keep the Eurozone together.

Not welcome

Angela visited Portugal and Greece in October 2012 to show support and unity, but she was not welcomed by the Greek public. There were violent protests upon her arrival. Many Greeks believed the austerity measures were too harsh and that Angela was to blame. Protestors held banners with images of Angela dressed in Nazi uniform or as a clown.

At the end of 2012, things were looking bleak for Europe and Angela. Will she and the EU be able to save the euro?

What next?

Few leaders have been re-elected during the economic crisis but Angela is one of them. She and her party are facing another general election in 2013.

Life as chancellor is not easy. Facing the media is just one of Angela's responsibilities.

Voter opinion

"Pragmatist" is a word often used to describe Angela. It means someone who deals with problems in a realistic way, rather than trying to stick rigidly to a particular point of view that might not work out. This is what Angela has done successfully and voters like her for it.

They like Angela because she is down-to-earth and willing to listen to all sides before making a decision. Like many German leaders, she has not always been able to achieve what she set out to do. However, in the German political system, compromise is essential or coalitions would break down.

Many politicians and journalists have underestimated Angela. She has said, "I've never underestimated myself. There's nothing wrong with being **ambitious**." *Time* magazine, 2010.

Most powerful woman

In 2012, Angela was announced as the world's most powerful woman by *Forbes* magazine for the second year running. In fact, she has been number one on the list for six out of the last seven years. Re-election in 2013 would probably see that trend continuing. Some people think that the CDU losing the 2013 election will mean Angela would disappear from politics altogether. We will have to wait and see.

Fight for freedom

Angela's childhood in East Germany provided her with a good background for politics. She says,

"I know what it is when you don't have freedom, and so I have a strong feeling for freedom, in comparison to the Western experience where the existence of freedom is normal, and fighting for it is not as necessary as it was for us."

Glossary

ambitious determined to succeed

analytical skills ability to think about difficult problems and suggest solutions

austerity describes government policies used during difficult economic conditions which can include spending cuts, tax increases, or a mixture of the two

bankrupt completely unable to pay money owed

boycott refuse to attend as a result of political views

cabinet group of senior ministers responsible for controlling government policy

campaign organized plan of how to achieve something, such as win an election

cabinet important members of a government, who work closely with the person in charge

candidate person who is put forward for a particular role or job

civilian person who is not a member of the armed forces

coalition two or more parties joining together to form a government

communism system in which the main resources of a society, such as factories and farms, are owned and controlled by the state. Wealth is distributed according to people's needs.

compromise when a person is prepared to give up something they want in order to reach an agreement with someone else

compulsory required or necessary

constituency voters in a particular area who vote for a representative to send to parliament or another law-making body

democracy system of government by the people, usually through chosen representatives

diplomacy skill of dealing with people in a sensitive and polite way

economy state of a country in terms of production of goods, spending on goods, and flow of money

European Union (EU) union of many European countries that works to increase the wealth and well-being of all citizens, and so they can move freely from one country to another. Sixteen EU members use the euro currency.

G8 summit meeting where officials from eight of the world's eleven top economies meet to discuss important global issues

general election voting in representatives from different areas of the country to parliament or another law-making body

inauguration official presentation of someone to a political role, such as chancellor

lenient go easy on someone or be generous towards them

margin in politics, an amount beyond what is needed to win an election

nominate officially put someone forward for a particular job

opposition party largest party that is not in power

pastor person in charge of a Christian church

policy overall plan to deal with running a country or organization

reunification process in 1990 in which the German Democratic Republic (GDR/East Germany) joined the Federal Republic of Germany (FRG/West Germany), and when Berlin reunited into a single city

ruthless showing no weakness when dealing with other people

taxes money paid to the government out of people's wages. Other taxes are added to the price of certain goods and services. Taxes pay for hospitals, schools, and other services.

underestimate think someone is less capable than they actually are

Timeline

1954	Angela Dorothea Kasner is born in Hamburg on 17 July
1973–1978	Angela attends the University of Leipzig where she studies physics
1977	Angela marries Ulrich Merkel
1978–1990	Angela works as a researcher at the Academy of Sciences in East Berlin
1982	Angela gets divorced from Ulrich Merkel
1986	Angela receives a PhD in physics from the University of Leipzig
1989	Angela becomes a member of the Democratic Awakening party
1990	Angela is made deputy spokesperson for the caretaker government in East Germany in February
1990	Angela joins the CDU (Christian Democratic Union) in August
1990	Reunification of Germany Angela becomes a member of the Bundestag in the first general election after reunification
1991–1994	Angela serves as Minister for Women and Youth
1991–1998	Angela is Deputy Chairwoman of the CDU
1994–1998	Angela serves as Minister for the Environment, Nature Conservation, and Nuclear Safety
1998	Angela marries for the second time, to Joachim Sauer
1998–2000	Angela is General Secretary of the CDU
2000	Angela is elected CDU president in April
2005	The CDU and CSU win the general election in coalition with the SPD
2005	Angela is sworn in as Chancellor on 22 November
2009	Angela's position as chancellor is renewed

Find out more

Books

Angela Merkel (Modern World Leaders), Clifford W. Mills (Chelsea House, 2007)

Germany (Countries Around the World), Mary Colson (Raintree, 2011)

The Berlin Wall (A Place in History), Anne Rooney (Franklin Watts, 2011)

Websites

europa.eu/about-eu/countries/member-countries/germany/index_en.htm
The European Union website has some interesting information about Germany.

news.bbc.co.uk/1/hi/world/europe/4572387.stm
This BBC web page is all about Angela Merkel.

Further research

If you want to find out more, here are a few topics you could investigate:
- Research the history of Germany, particularly around World War II.
- Try to learn more about the German political system and decide whether you think it is a good system.
- Research other women leaders in the 20th and 21st centuries.

Index